BETTY

THE HELEN BETTY OSBORNE STORY

WRITTEN BY DAVID A. ROBERTSON

ILLUSTRATED BY SCOTT B. HENDERSON

HIGHWATER PRESS

We acknowledge the support of the Canada Council for the Arts.
Nous remercions le Conseil des arts du Canada de son soutien.

HighWater Press gratefully acknowledges the financial support of the Province of Manitoba through the Department of Sport, Culture and Heritage and the Manitoba Book Publishing Tax Credit, and the Government of Canada through the Canada Book Fund (CBF), for our publishing activities.

HighWater Press is an imprint of Portage & Main Press.
Printed and bound in Canada by Friesens
Design by Relish New Brand Experience

For close to 1,200 missing and murdered Indigenous women in Canada, that they be honoured and not ignored. —D.A.R.

Library and Archives Canada Cataloguing in Publication

Robertson, David, 1977-, author
Betty : the Helen Betty Osborne story / David Alexander Robertson ; illustrated by Scott B. Henderson.

Issued in print and electronic formats.
ISBN 978-1-55379-544-5 (pbk.).--ISBN 978-1-55379-545-2 (pdf).--
ISBN 978-1-55379-546-9 (epub)

1. Osborne, Helen Betty, 1952-1971--Comic books, strips, etc. 2. Osborne, Helen Betty, 1952-1971--Juvenile literature. 3. Native women--Crimes against--Canada--Comic books, strips, etc. 4. Native women--Crimes against--Canada--Juvenile literature. 5. Native women--Violence against--Canada--Comic books, strips, etc. 6. Native women--Violence against--Canada--Juvenile literature. 7. Graphic novels. I. Henderson, Scott B., illustrator II. Title.

E98.W8R63 2015 j362.83'9997071 C2015-902147-2
C2015-902148-0

23 22 21 20 3 4 5 6 7

www.highwaterpress.com
Winnipeg, Manitoba
Treaty 1 Territory and homeland of the Métis Nation

Facebook

https://www.facebook.com

Google Images Google Search Pinterest Facebook Twitter

Aiden | Home

Cheryl Brown
40 mins

Hey everyone! My daughter is selling Girl Guide cookies again w/ her troop! The chocolate mint kind. :/ Yuck, but 4 a good cause! $5/box. Get urs b4 we go door2door!

Like • Comment • Share

Sandy Irvine 4 Sure cuz!
39 mins • Like

Kent Gordon Gross.
15 mins • Like

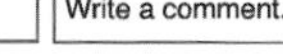

Write a comment...

DJ Green
41 mins

Good morning y'all! Looks like the Leafs are driving to the Cup this year!

Like • Comment • Share

Mark Fontaine a boy can (day) dream

Write a comment...

Alan Todd
43 mins

won a bonus game on myVEGAS Slots.

Suggested Pages

David Robertson Commented on Francis Eyers' post.

Scott Henderson posted a photo.

Annalee Greenberg likes Kirsten's link.

Pam Snowbird going to play ball later. Who's up? **Keenan**?

Niigaanwewedam James Sinclair shared **Tina's** post.

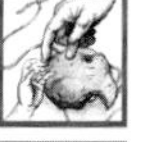

Daniel Hey, **April**, wish your Kookum a happy birthday from me!

Lauren Blackbird was tagged in Julia Moore's photo.

Cole GreyEyes shared a

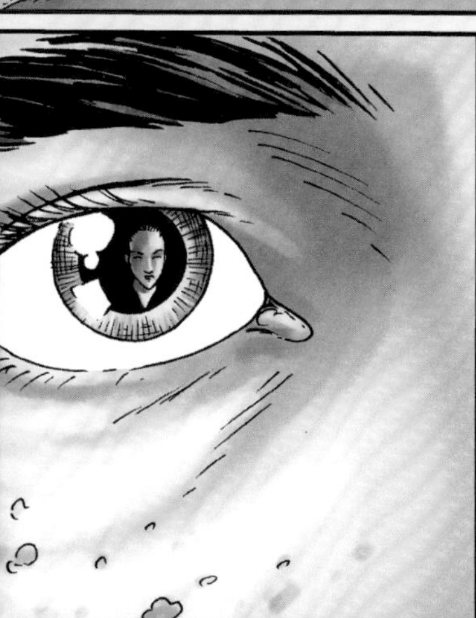

Francis Eyers shared **Missing Manitoba Women's** post
45 mins

Is it just me, or do these come up, like, every fricking day? What the heck?

Winnipeg Police Renew request for public assistance to locate 16 year old Amanda Sinclair. Was last seen Nov. 8 in Osborne Village area. Sinclair is around five-foot-five-inches tall, weighs 160 pounds, has long brown hair... See More

23 Likes • 93 Comments • Share

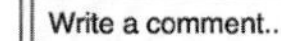

Write a comment...

CLICK

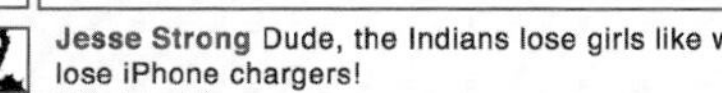

Jesse Strong Dude, the Indians lose girls like we lose iPhone chargers!
29 mins • Like

Jeff Armstrong Horrible. What's going on?
27 mins • Like

Helen Tapper What happens to all the Aboriginal women? Where do they go? Who is taking them? Prayers out
27 mins • Like

Andrea Smith NO REASON for you people to be roaming the streets like ANIMALS! GET A JOB!!!...Go to school and pay your own way!!..Or head on back to your reserve! GIVE YOUR HEADS

Edwin Blackbird commented on James Blackbird's photo.

Catherine Gerbasi likes McNally Robinson Bookstores.

Kirsten Phillips shared a photo.

Pamela Greene is going to **Kathy Richardson's recital.**

Jesse Strong commented on Kathy Richardson's event.

Kathy Richardson shared an event **Kathy's Poetry Recital.**

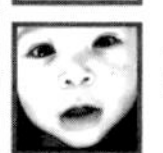

Jill Robertson shared **David Robertson's** link.

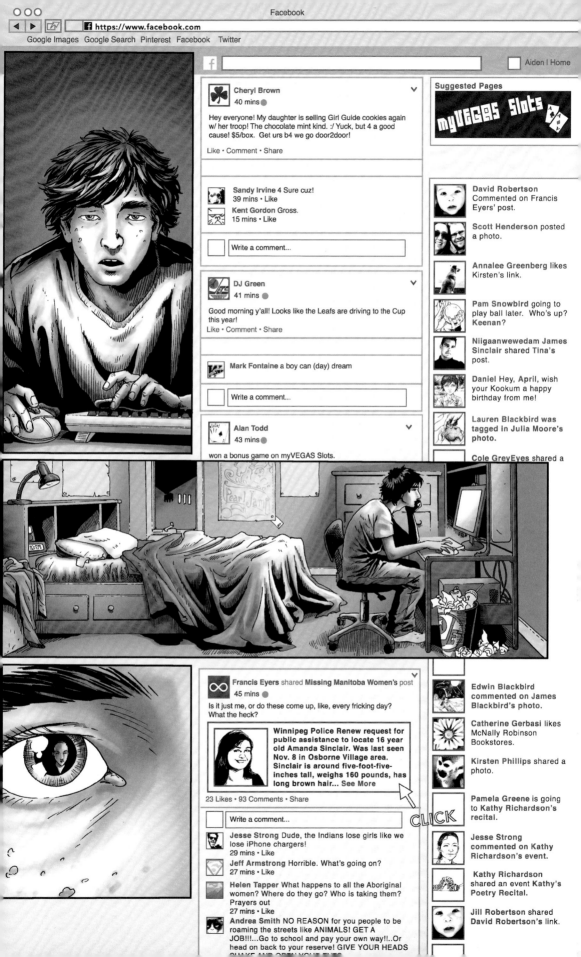

http://www.nwac.ca
Google Images Google Search Pinterest Facebook Twitter
MISSING AND MURDERED
INDIGENOUS WOMEN
IN CANADA

BETTY

THE HELEN BETTY OSBORNE STORY

WRITTEN BY DAVID A. ROBERTSON

ILLUSTRATED BY SCOTT B. HENDERSON

EARLIER...

WHAT DO WE WANT?

JUSTICE!!!

WHEN DO WE WANT IT?

NOW!!!

STOP

AM I NEXT?

ABORIGINAL WOMEN ARE LOVED AND VALUED

MURDERER

WHAT IF SHE WAS YOUR DAUGHTER?

HONK! HONK! HONK! HONK! HONK! HONK! HONK! HONK! HONK! HONK! HONK!

WE ARE HERE TODAY BECAUSE YET ANOTHER ONE OF OUR SISTERS IS GONE.

HEY BETTY, I THOUGHT YOU'D BE PACKING. WE LEAVE TOMORROW, IN CASE YOU FORGOT.*
I'M PACKED.
*THEY SPEAK IN THE SWAMPY CREE DIALECT.

ARE YOU SCARED?
SCARED?
NO. NERVOUS MAYBE. I'VE BEEN AWAY FROM HOME BEFORE, JUST NOT *AWAY*.
I KNOW...

BUT BEING SCARED OR NERVOUS SHOULDN'T KEEP US FROM GOING. WE KNOW WHAT WE WANT TO BE, RIGHT?
TEACHERS.
AND THAT'S THE EXACT REASON WHY WE HAVE TO LEAVE.

KIDS SHOULDN'T HAVE TO LEAVE HOME TO GO TO SCHOOL. WHEN WE'RE TEACHERS, EVA, WE'LL COME BACK HERE AND MAKE SURE THEY NEVER HAVE TO. TOMORROW'S JUST A LONG TRIP TO GET BACK HOME.

KAWAPAMEKAWEN, NEKAWE.*

*SEE YOU, MOTHER.

THE PAS AIRPORT.

I'LL BE GLAD WHEN MY FEET TOUCH THE GROUND.
ME TOO.

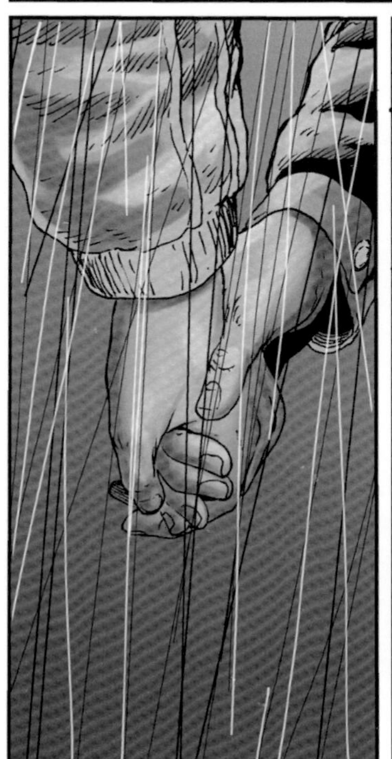

GUY HILL RESIDENTIAL SCHOOL, 1971.

HI.
HEY BETTY.

I LIKE THE DARK BACK HOME.
ME TOO.
IT'S SMALLER HERE, LIKE THERE'S NO ROOM FOR ANYTHING ELSE.

DO YOU KNOW WHAT I FIND, THOUGH?
WHAT'S THAT?
THE LONGER YOU'RE IN THE DARKNESS, THE LESS SCARY IT IS.

EKOSI, BETTY.
SURE.

WHAT ARE YOU WRITING? IT'S ALL YOU'VE BEEN DOING ALL DAY.

BETTY?
THEY WANT TO SEND ME BACK HOME. THEY SAY MY GRADES AREN'T GOOD ENOUGH.

WHAT?
BUT WHAT ABOUT US? WHAT ABOUT BEING TEACHERS?
WE *WILL* BE.
BUT YOU SAID THEY'RE GOING TO SEND YOU HOME.

I SAID THEY WANT TO. I'M NOT GOING ANYWHERE. THAT'S WHAT I'VE BEEN WRITING.
WHAT IS IT?
A LETTER.

"I DO NOT KNOW WHAT TO DO IF I GO HOME. I'D RATHER GO TO SCHOOL AND MY MOM IS NOT STAYING WITH THE FAMILY ANYMORE. I JUST HAVE A PLACE TO STAY FOR THE HOLIDAYS."
"I'LL DO MY BEST. PLEASE GIVE ME A CHANCE TO GO TO SCHOOL AT THE PAS IN SEPTEMBER. I'LL DO MY VERY BEST. PLEASE. YOURS TRULY, BETTY OSBORNE."
SEE?
THAT SOUNDS GOOD.

THERE'S NOTHING TO WORRY ABOUT.
WE'LL BE IN THE PAS COME THE FALL.

BENSON HOUSEHOLD.
NOVEMBER 12, 1971, 6:00PM.

WOULD YOU PLEASE PASS THE SALT?
CERTAINLY.
THANKS.

DO YOU HAVE ANY PLANS TONIGHT?
NOT REALLY. I'M GOING TO HEAD OVER TO ST. ANTHONY'S TO SEE A FRIEND FROM SCHOOL.

OH, I HOPE THEY AREN'T TOO SICK.
NO, SHE'S OKAY. SHE'S GOT THE FLU OR SOMETHING.

MAY I BE EXCUSED?
YES.

ST. ANTHONY'S HOSPITAL. 7:00PM.
BETTY?

HEY GEORGE, WHAT ARE YOU UP TO?
NOT MUCH, YOU?
SAME.
JUST POPPED IN ON SARAH.
HOW'S SHE DOING?
BETTER. HEY, WANT TO COME OVER?
SURE, YEAH.

TELEPHONE
HELLO?
OH HI, MRS. BENSON.
CAN I BRING A FRIEND OVER?
I DON'T SEE WHY NOT.
THANKS.

LET'S GO.

COLGAN HOUSEHOLD. 8:00PM.
DAD, CAN I HAVE THE CAR TONIGHT?
NOT TONIGHT.
BUD, JUST LET HIM HAVE IT.
YEAH, DAD, LEMME HAVE IT. I'M NOT GOIN' ANYWHERE WITH IT, REALLY.
FINE, FINE, TAKE IT.
HA!
JIM, HOW ABOUT A NIGHT ON THE TOWN!
TO DO WHAT?
WHAT ELSE IS THERE TO DO ON FRIDAYS, MAN? DRINK AND GET LAID.
SOUNDS BETTER THAN NOTHING.
YEAH!
LET'S GO!!
VRRRRRRMMMMMM!

BENSON HOUSEHOLD.
10:00PM.
YOU DIDN'T.
I DID.
I STEPPED RIGHT THERE IN THE MIDDLE OF BOTH OF THEM AND TOLD THEM TO STOP FIGHTING. AND YOU KNOW WHAT?
THEY DID.
BETTY OSBORNE, HA.
THEY SHOULD'VE KNOWN BETTER.
"THOUGH SHE BE BUT LITTLE, SHE IS FIERCE."

I LIKE THAT.
BUT FIERCE IN A NICE WAY.
OF COURSE.
OF COURSE.

BETTY, IT'S TIME TO STOP. NO MORE DRINKING, GOT IT?
YES.
SORRY, MRS. BENSON.

I THOUGHT ABOUT GOING TO THE STORE FOR SOME SNACKS. IS THAT OKAY?
YOU MIGHT FREEZE OUT THERE, YOU TWO.
OH, IT'S NOT BAD. IT'S WAY COLDER BACK HOME.
WELL, I SUPPOSE SO. I CAN FINISH UP HERE.

I THINK MRS. BENSON COULD BREAK UP A FIGHT BETTER THAN YOU, MY FRIEND.
SHE AND MR. BENSON, ARE GOOD PEOPLE.
BUT ARE THEY NICE?
OH YEAH. NICE, LIKE ME.
OF COURSE.
HA.
OF COURSE.

COLGAN VEHICLE.
11:00PM.
CRAP!
WE'RE OUT BOYS. GOTTA STOCK UP.
I DON'T HAVE ANY CASH.
ME NEITHER.
NORM, YOU NEVER GOT ANY CASH.
WAIT, WAIT, WAIT!
I'VE GOT AN IDEA!

JUST HANG ON, I'LL BE RIGHT BACK.
HURRY UP, I'M GETTING DAMN THIRSTY!

WAKE UP! WAKE UP! WAKE UP!
HEY!
ANYBODY HOME!?

KNOCK KNOCK!!!
CRASH!

DEVIL'S WINE, BABY!
WHOOOO!
VERY GOOD. NOW SHUT UP BEFORE YOU WAKE UP THE WHOLE CITY!

THE CAMBRIAN HOTEL.
11:00PM.
WHERE TO?
I...

CORNY?
BETTY, I...

WHO IS THIS?
ARE YOU CHEATING ON ME?
WHO?
HER?
NO!
HER?

DON'T LIE TO ME.
ARE YOU OR NOT?
SPEAK FOR YOUR-SELF, OUT WITH ANOTHER GUY.
DON'T CHANGE THE SUBJECT. YOU KNOW GEORGE IS ONLY A FRIEND AND THAT I LOVE YOU.
AND I LOVE YOU!
JEEZ!

COME ON, GEORGE. LET'S GO!
WHERE? GETTING SNACKS?
BETTY!
I'M NOT THAT HUNGRY ANYMORE.

THE NORTHERN LITE CAFÉ. 11:10 PM.
HEY GUYS.
HEY BETTY, WHAT'S WRONG?
DON'T ASK.

11:20 PM.
WHERE ARE WE HEADED?
WE CAN GO BACK TO THE BENSON'S.
BUT WE GOT KICKED OUT.
WE CAN HANG OUT IN THE SHED.

THE ROYAL CANADIAN LEGION. 11:55PM.
PASS IT OVER HERE, MAN.
JUST WAIT A SEC, JEE-ZUS.

WELL, WE GOT THE DRINKING OUT OF THE WAY, EH JIM?
I'D SAY SO.
UHHHH...

WHERE DOES THAT LEAVE US, LEE?
TIME TO GET LAID, MAN! THAT'S HOW YOU CAP OFF A FRIDAY NIGHT.
LET'S DO IT!

EVER REGRET WRITING THAT LETTER, BETTY?
NO.
SOMETIMES I WISH I'D BEEN SENT HOME.
I MEAN, I GET HOMESICK. WE ALL DO.

BUT I THINK I'M RIGHT WHERE I'M SUPPOSED TO BE.
MAYBE WE ALL ARE, HEY?
YEAH.

WHAT TIME IS IT, ANYWAY?
MIDNIGHT.
AH, BETTER BE HEADING HOME.
ME TOO.

SEE YOU MONDAY.
OR SOONER.
BYE, GUYS.

NOVEMBER 13, 1971.
12:00AM.
WANT TO HEAD OVER TO THE DANCE?
I'M SURPRISED WE HAVEN'T GONE YET. ISN'T THAT KIND OF YOUR THING?
I DO LOVE TO DANCE. I'M GOING TO DANCE ALL MY TROUBLES AWAY.
YOU KNOW, THINGS'LL BE FINE WITH CORNY.
YEAH, I KNOW.

12:30AM.

YOU KNOW WHAT?
I BETTER GET HOME. I'VE HAD ENOUGH EXCITEMENT FOR ONE NIGHT.
THAT WAS EXCITING TO YOU? YOU DON'T GET OUT MUCH.
HA HA.
IT'S ALL RIGHT, I'LL SEE YOU MONDAY.

SEE YA, BETTY.
BYE.
OH, HOW I WISH WE WERE BACK ON THE ROAD AGAIN. ME AND YOU AND A DOG NAMED BOO, TRAVELLIN' AND LIVIN' OFF THE LAND...

ME AND YOU AND A DOG NAMED BOO, HOW I LOVE BEING A FREE...

THE CAMBRIAN HOTEL. 12:45AM.
THE ROYAL CANADIAN LEGION. 2:00AM.

2:00AM.

HEY, THERE'S DWAYNE!
NO WAY. LET'S PICK HIM UP.
HEY DWAYNE!
DWAYNE!!
GET OVER HERE!
HONK! HONK! HONK!

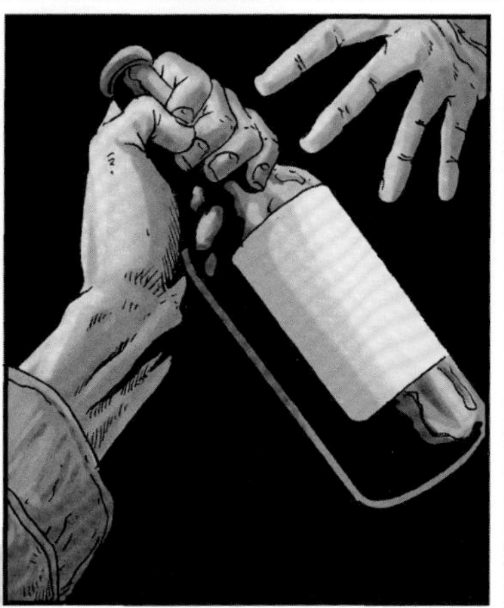

EDWARDS AVENUE.
2:15AM.

HELLO, BETTY!

3RD STREET WEST.
2:30AM.

HEY, YOU WANNA COME PARTY?
WE GOT SOME WINE. I KNOW YOU WANT SOME.

COME ON, COME PARTY WITH US.
NO.

ISN'T "NO" INDIAN FOR "YES"?
YOU KNOW, I THINK YOU'RE RIGHT. INDIAN GIRLS DON'T SAY NO.

NO!
LET GO!!
LET'S GO POCAHONTAS!
NO!!!
GET HER, DWAYNE!

HOUGHTON FAMILY CABIN.

HELP!! SOMEBODY PLEASE!!
HA HA HA HA HA HEH HEH HA HEH
HA HA HA HA HA HEH HEH
HA HA HA HEH HA
HEH HEH HA HA HA
HELP ME!!

HEY, SHUT HER UP.

HELP ME!!!
HELP ME PLEASE!!!
SHUT UP!
WE HAVE TO GET HER OUT OF HERE. WE'RE GOING TO GET CAUGHT.
THIS WAS SUPPOSED TO BE EASY.
SHE WAS SUPPOSED TO BE EASY.

I KNOW WHERE TO TAKE HER.

NOBODY'LL HEAR HER.

PUMP HOUSE.

GET OUT!
YOU CAN'T DO THIS!
OH YEAH? WHO'S STOPPING ME?

I'M GOING TO TELL THE POLICE!
YOU'RE NOT TELLING ANYONE.
THUD!

JIM, GET OUT HERE!

CRAP.
COMING.

SLAM

THUD
STOP!
PLEASE!
HOLD HER DOWN.
SLAP
YOU THINK YOU'RE GONNA TALK?
THUD
SOMEBODY HELP!!
HELP ME!!
KEEP HER THERE.
I GOT HER.
WHAT ARE YOU DOING?
SHUT UP.
STOP.
PLEASE.
THUMP
THUMP
THUMP
THUMP
THUMP
THUMP

THE NEXT MORNING.

THOSE WHO ABDUCTED HER SHOWED A TOTAL LACK OF REGARD FOR HER PERSON OR HER RIGHTS AS AN INDIVIDUAL.
THOSE WHO STOOD BY WHILE THE PHYSICAL ASSAULT TOOK PLACE...SHOWED THEIR OWN RACISM, SEXISM, AND INDIFFERENCE.
THOSE WHO KNEW THE STORY AND REMAINED SILENT MUST SHARE THEIR GUILT.

...BUT WHAT CAN WE DO?

WELL, IT'S A START...
Winnipeg Police Renew request fo
public assistance to locate 16 ye
old Amanda Sinclair. Was last se
Nov. 8 in Osborne Village area.
Sinclair is around five-foot-five-
inches tall, weighs 160 pounds,
long brown hair... See More
23 Likes • 93 Comments • Share
Write a comment...
Jesse Strong Dude, the Indians lose girls
lose iPhone chargers!
29 mins • Like
Jeff Armstrong Horrible. What's going o
27 mins • Like
Helen Tapper What happens to all the
Where do they go? Who is tak

hes tall, we
g brown h
s • Share
CLICK